THE POCKET
MOON MAGIC

Published in 2025
by Gemini Books
Part of Gemini Books Group

Based in Woodbridge and London

Marine House, Tide Mill Way
Woodbridge, Suffolk IP12 1AP
United Kingdom
www.geminibooks.com

Text and Design © 2025 Gemini Adult Books Ltd
Part of the Gemini Pockets series

Cover image: Shutterstock Ltd/Benny Marty

ISBN 978-1-80247-280-6

All rights reserved. No part of this publication may be reproduced in any form or by any means – electronic, mechanical, photocopying, recording or otherwise – or stored in any retrieval system of any nature without prior written permission from the copyright holders.

A CIP catalogue record for this book is available from the British Library.

Disclaimer: The book is a guidebook purely for information and entertainment purposes only. All trademarks, individual and company names, brand names, registered names, quotations, celebrity names, logos, dialogues and catchphrases used or cited in this book are the property of their respective owners. The publisher does not assume and hereby disclaims any liability to any party for any loss, damage or disruption caused by errors or omissions, whether such errors or omissions result from negligence, accident or any other cause. This book is an unofficial and unauthorized publication by Gemini Adult Books Ltd and has not been licensed, approved, sponsored or endorsed by any person or entity.

Printed in China

10 9 8 7 6 5 4 3 2 1

Images: Shutterstock: 2 /Benny Marty; 35, 55, 77, 91, 95, 107, 127 /Marish; 12, 13, 14, 17, 18, 21, 25, 26, 29, 61 /Minur; 4, 8, 30, 56, 94, 128 /lyubava.21; 3, 8, 30, 41 /DASHADD. Freepik: 33, 37, 49, 65, 69, 73, 108, 121; 83 /Macrovector.

THE POCKET

MOON MAGIC

Harness the power of the lunar cycle

CONTENTS

Introduction   06

CHAPTER ONE
Moon Manifestation   08

CHAPTER TWO
Harness the Power of the Moon   30

CHAPTER THREE
Moon Rituals   56

CHAPTER FOUR
Lunar Spells   94

Introduction

Whether you've recently found yourself noticing the soothing presence of the Moon or are seeking ways to deepen its role in your life, this book has something for you.

Pocket-sized and easy-to-use, *Moon Magic* reveals the secrets of each lunar phase and gives tips on how to harness the Moon's power. It teaches you how to manifest with the lunar cycle as well as how to use crystals, herbs and essential oils to amplify the Moon's energy.

Simple step-by-step rituals and spells will help you add more magic to your daily life and connect with the unique rhythms and energies of the lunar phases.

> **Heavenly witness, that the Moon saw you and wished to see more.**

John Milton,
Paradise Lost (1674)

Chapter One
MOON MANIFESTATION

What is the Moon?

The Moon is a celestial body (a natural object in space) that lights our night sky by reflecting light from the Sun. We only see one side of it because it rotates in sync with its slightly tilted and elliptical orbit around Earth.

The Moon affects life on Earth in many ways; for example, owls and bats are influenced by moonlight and many people believe that plant growth is affected by the lunar phases. The Moon governs ocean tides due to its gravitational pull – and humans are impacted, too, as our bodies are made up of around 60 per cent water.

For many, the Moon's phases directly affect their emotions. For example, some feel hot and fiery at the Full Moon and then quiet and introspective at the New Moon. Do you notice similar feelings at certain points of the lunar cycle?

MOON MANIFESTATION

Buy or download a lunar calendar to help you track each phase. Keep a diary to see if you spot any patterns in your energy or emotions that mirror the Moon's.

Lunar eclipses, which occur when the Earth passes between the Sun and the Moon, take place multiple times a year during a Full Moon.

MOON MANIFESTATION

Phases of the Moon

The Moon goes through a cycle of phases over 29.5 days. Each phase lasts around 3 days.

These are the main phases:

- New Moon
- Waxing Crescent Moon
- First Quarter Moon
- Waxing Gibbous Moon
- Full Moon
- Waning Gibbous Moon
- Last Quarter Moon
- Waning Crescent Moon

MOON MAGIC

New Moon

The New Moon marks the very beginning of the lunar cycle. As the Moon is not visible from Earth at this phase, it represents the potential for transformation.

It is the perfect time to set intentions and focus on new creative projects, career goals or personal growth. An intention is a statement of what you want to manifest in your life. It gives you a specific outcome to direct your energy and actions toward.

In some traditions, people release negative energy at this time. One way to do this is to write down anything that is no longer serving you – such as fear, negative thoughts or self-doubt – and then safely burn the paper. The burning is a symbolic act of release.

MOON MANIFESTATION

In Chinese folklore, the Moon is home to Chang'e, a goddess who took refuge there after drinking an elixir of immortality that she stole from her husband.

Artemis was the Greek goddess of both the Moon and the hunt. She is often associated with the protection of women.

MOON MANIFESTATION

Waxing Crescent Moon

The Waxing Crescent Moon symbolizes growth and rising energy. It's a time to build momentum and nurture the intentions set during the New Moon.

During this phase, take concrete steps toward your goals. If your intention is to drink more water, this is the time to create supportive habits – like placing a water bottle on your bedside table, on your desk and in your bag. Taking aligned action like this is crucial when manifesting as the energy of this phase is highly supportive.

Use this time to engage in spells and rituals that help you create good habits, learn skills and build resources that lead to your goals.

First Quarter Moon

The First Quarter Moon, when half of the Moon is illuminated, symbolizes overcoming obstacles.

It's common for barriers or conflicts to appear quite soon after setting an intention. For instance, if you aim to take on more leadership at work, a situation may arise that makes you doubt your abilities.

This can be seen as the Universe testing your commitment and offering opportunities to release old, stagnant energies that hinder your goals. By facing these obstacles in this phase, you can shed the beliefs that are incompatible with your goals, and this allows you to take positive action.

The First Quarter Moon is ideal for spells and rituals focused on breaking down barriers, resolving conflicts, confronting fears and making brave decisions.

In ancient Greece, the goddess Selene personified the Moon, and was believed to ride through the night sky in a silver chariot.

Luna is the Roman equivalent of Selene. She represents the embodiment of moonlight.

MOON MANIFESTATION

Waxing Gibbous Moon

As the Moon grows closer to being full, the Waxing Gibbous Moon invites us to pause and assess whether we need to adjust our plans for manifesting our goals.

For example, if you set an intention to start a new exercise routine, you may realize that something needs to change for you to stay on track. Perhaps you need to adjust the time of day that you fit in your workouts or maybe you need a gentler form of exercise.

This phase is excellent for practising magic that enhances your focus and efficiency.

Full Moon

The Full Moon represents the peak of the lunar cycle. It is a time of completion and is the most powerful phase for manifestation. This is because the Moon's energy is at its greatest!

There are typically 12 Full Moons each year, though sometimes there can be 13. Occasionally, a Blue Moon occurs. This is when two Full Moons occur within one month.

The Full Moon is a potent time for performing magic related to protection and divination (foreseeing the future using tools such as Tarot).

Full Moon rituals can involve expressing gratitude, releasing what no longer serves us and celebrating our achievements.

MOON MANIFESTATION

Native American tribes named each Full Moon to reflect the seasonal changes specific to their culture and environment.

The Waning Gibbous phase is an excellent time for spells and rituals focused on gratitude, generosity and imparting wisdom.

MOON MANIFESTATION

Waning Gibbous Moon

The Waning Gibbous phase occurs after the Full Moon, as the Moon begins to reduce in size, or wane. This period symbolizes reflection, gratitude and the sharing of knowledge.

The Moon's energy during this time is calming, making it ideal for reflecting on the previous phases and giving back to others – if you have been working on personal growth, this is when you might share what you have recently learned with a friend or loved one.

MOON MAGIC

Last Quarter Moon

The left half of the Moon is illuminated during the Last Quarter Moon. This phase is ideal for reassessing and clearing space.

If you've been holding onto a grudge or a habit that is no longer beneficial, this is a potent time to release it. You might choose a simple burning ritual as suggested during the New Moon (*see page 14*) or opt for other forgiveness and purification practices.

Magic during the Last Quarter Moon is powerful for banishing negativity and fostering forgiveness.

MOON MANIFESTATION

The Egyptian goddess Isis is often linked to the Moon due to her association with magic and healing.

Tsukuyomi is the Japanese Shinto Moon god who rules over the night.

MOON MANIFESTATION

Waning Crescent Moon

The Waning Crescent Moon is the final phase of the lunar cycle. At this time, the Moon appears as a thin crescent. This phase encourages rest, renewal and preparation for the new cycle that is soon to begin with another New Moon.

It is a perfect time for spells and rituals that focus on rest and healing, especially if you have been feeling particularly stressed out or drained.

Practices during this phase can include meditation, reflection and cleansing rituals to build up your energy.

Chapter Two

HARNESS THE POWER OF THE MOON

Writing a New Moon intention

To write a New Moon intention, start by reflecting on what it is that you truly want to manifest in your life during this lunar cycle and beyond. You can ask yourself this question while you meditate, journal or go for a walk to connect with what feels most important. Focus on the core feelings you wish to experience so you know that it comes from your heart.

Write or speak your intentions using clear, positive language in the present tense. For example, "I am mindful," instead of, "I want to be more mindful." Be specific and focus on what you want to invite, not avoid.

HARNESS THE POWER OF THE MOON

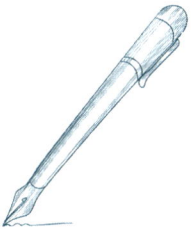

Next, visualize your intentions as though they are already true, connecting deeply with the emotions this evokes.

Lastly, release your attachment to the outcome by choosing to trust that the Universe will bring your desires to fruition in the best way – and that you may not know what that will be!

For example: "I am fully supported in my feminine power as I attract abundant opportunities to grow my business."

TOP TIP: Keep a spell and ritual journal to record your experiences.

Calm your mind

Preparing your mind is an important first step in harnessing the power of the Moon. Having a clear mental state helps you connect more deeply with the lunar energies.

Techniques such as meditation, breathing exercises and visualization can help you relax and focus.

A very simple meditation involves sitting or lying down comfortably and quietly focusing on your breath to let your thoughts pass by, like clouds in the sky. With practice, even just a few minutes can help you feel calmer and more relaxed.

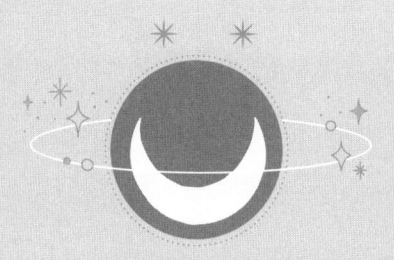

Breathing exercises, such as deep belly breathing, can help the body access the parasympathetic nervous system (also called rest and digest).

Visualization is a great way to help your mind prepare for success – many athletes use it before competitive events. It involves imagining your desired outcomes as though they have already happened.

Moon meditation

This simple meditation will help deepen your connection to the Full Moon. If you can't go outside to do it, simply use your imagination.

On a dry night, find a safe and comfortable place to sit outside. Close your eyes or gaze a few metres ahead. Begin taking deep, slow breaths.

With each breath, imagine seeing yourself from above, sitting quietly in your chosen spot.

Imagine travelling higher – now you can see your road, then town or city. Continue rising higher and higher until you pass through a layer of cool, soft clouds.

Visualize yourself above the clouds. The bright, Full Moon is enormous in the night sky and is bathing everything in its healing silver light.

HARNESS THE POWER OF THE MOON

Relax into this magical space and breathe in the gentle, nurturing moonlight.

Silently ask the Moon if there is any message that it wishes to share with you. If you receive any insights, thank the Moon for its wisdom.

When you're ready, slowly come back down to your body and once you feel fully present, open your eyes.

Simple breathing

Try this breathing exercise before your spell or ritual work to bring clarity and calm.

Find somewhere quiet and comfortable to sit and set a timer with a gentle alarm. If you like, play some instrumental, rhythmical music.

Start by slowly inhaling through your nose for a count of four. Focus on letting go of any tension – mental or physical. Now hold your breath for a count of four. Exhale through your mouth, for another count of four. And hold on the out-breath for a count of four. Repeat this pattern five times.

HARNESS THE POWER OF THE MOON

Rhiannon is a Celtic goddess linked to the Moon, horses and forgiveness.

Moonlight visualization

This visualization helps you align your energy with the Moon's supportive power, creating a strong foundation for your spell and ritual work.

Begin by sitting comfortably. Close your eyes and take several deep breaths. Imagine the dark night sky above you, with stars twinkling and the bright Moon shining down. Visualize the Moon's light flowing gently down into the top of your head.

Feel the moonlight slowly moving through your body and filling you with a deep sense of peace. Then guide the moonlight to your heart, where it forms a beautiful orb of silver light. Silently speak your intention.

Let the orb of moonlight expand, filling your entire being with feelings of empowerment and success. Imagine the light dissolving anything that is blocking your manifestation.

Now, visualize yourself as though your intention has already come true, feeling the strength and support of the Moon as you do so. When you are ready, open your eyes.

Preparing your body

Physical preparation for moon magic can include grounding, wearing loose, comfortable clothes, taking ritual baths and purifying your space.

Wearing soft and loose clothing allows you to maintain your focus – make sure to avoid anything tight or itchy.

Grounding techniques can help balance your energy – try walking or standing barefoot on natural ground or some light stretching or yoga.

Ritual baths are warm baths with herbs, flowers, salts or essential oils. You can imagine the water cleansing your body and spirit as you soak – then draining away as you let out the water.

Purifying with herbs

Burning herbs such as rosemary, lavender and thyme can cleanse and purify your body and environment. They do this by absorbing and carrying away any negative energy through the smoke.

Always be mindful of where the herbs you use come from to remain respectful of different cultures and traditions, and ideally use herbs that are grown locally to you.

Once you have chosen your herbs, prepare them for burning. Bundle them tightly with twine, and then hang somewhere to dry for one to two weeks. When they are ready, set an intention for cleansing, then safely light the bundle and let the smoke purify your energy or space.

Light yoga for grounding

These three simple yoga poses are brilliant for grounding as they help cultivate a sense of centeredness and balance.

Mountain pose

Stand with your feet roughly hip-width apart. Feel your feet on the ground and notice how the Earth is supporting you. Imagine roots growing down from the soles of your feet to the centre of the Earth. Lift your head to lengthen your spine, roll your shoulders back and allow your arms to hang down by your sides. Take a few deep breaths.

Tree pose

Standing, shift your weight to your left foot and make sure it is placed firmly on the ground. Slowly lift your right foot and place it on the inside of your left thigh. If that is too tricky, try just above your ankle (avoid pressing on your knee). Place your hands together over your heart, take some deep breaths then repeat on the other side.

Standing forward fold

Slowly fold forward from standing until your hands reach as close to the ground as you comfortably can, hinging at your hips. Breathe deeply a few times, then come back up to standing.

MOON MAGIC

In the Yoruba tradition of West Africa, the protective, nurturing deity Yemoja is linked to the Moon, as well as to fertility, motherhood, rivers and creation.

Barefoot grounding

This powerful grounding activity can be done barefoot or wearing socks, indoors or outdoors. It can also be done sitting in a chair with your feet firmly planted on the floor. But if possible, go outside and stand barefoot on some grass.

Close your eyes and imagine roots going down from the soles of your feet deep into the Earth.

Imagine any stress or negativity that you are holding moving out of your body, down these roots into the Earth, where it is recycled as life-giving energy.

Imagine this new energy travelling back up the roots and flowing through your body, filling you with a sense of calm, stability and renewed strength.

Setting up a simple altar

An altar is a special place or surface (such as a shelf or small tabletop) where you can focus your energy during spell and ritual work.

Many traditions include items that represent the four elements – earth, air, fire and water – to balance the energy of the altar. For earth, you might use crystals, gemstones or flowers. Air can be symbolized by incense or feathers, while candles are a common representation of fire. Water can be represented by seashells or by a simple bowl of water, possibly charged by being placed in direct moonlight.

Most altars have a special cloth or piece of fabric upon which you place the items. You can also add photos, statues or other personal tokens that symbolize whatever you wish to manifest.

Candle care

- Ideally use a new candle for each new spell or ritual.

- To anoint a candle with oil, rub it into the candle while focusing on your intention. If you want to attract something, rub the oil from the top of the candle to its base. To repel something, rub the oil from the base of the candle to its top.

- Blowing out a candle is thought to blow away your intention – so safely let it burn out or use a candle snuffer to close your ritual or spell.

Choosing colours

As you select items for your altar, consciously choose the colours of your cloths, candles, crystals and other items based on their symbolic meanings.

- **White** for clarity and peace.
- **Silver** for intuition and feminine energy.
- **Blue** for healing, communication and wisdom.
- **Black** for protection and removing negativity.
- **Purple** for transformation.
- **Green** for growth, abundance and fertility.
- **Red** for added passion, courage and strength.
- **Yellow** for joy, creativity and clarity.
- **Pink** for love, compassion and joy.
- **Gold** for success, abundance and confidence.
- **Brown** for grounding and a connection to nature.
- **Orange** for creativity and success.

*Choosing colours
that align with
your intention can
enhance the energy
you are creating.*

MOON MAGIC

Most crystals need regular cleansing to recharge their energy. To do this, place them somewhere dry outside (or on a windowsill) for a few hours under a Full Moon.

Crystals & gemstones

Crystals and gemstones can amplify the power of moon magic. You can use crystals in your spell and ritual work by holding them or by placing them on your altar.

- **Moonstone** strengthens your intuition.
- **Silver Quartz** boosts the power of intentions.
- **Selenite** creates a peaceful space.
- **Labradorite** enhances personal transformation.
- **Black Obsidian** protects you from negativity.
- **Tourmaline** provides protection.
- **Amethyst** encourages calm.
- **Citrine** attracts abundance.

Herbs & oils

Incorporate these natural elements into your spells and rituals by placing them on your altar. You can burn dried herbs on charcoal discs in a fire-safe incense burner and place the essential oils in an oil burner or a diffuser.

Herbs

- **Lavender** promotes calm.
- **Peppermint** boosts energy.
- **Basil** attracts good fortune.
- **Rose** promotes love and healing.
- **Lemon balm** supports healing.
- **Mugwort** enhances intuition.

Essential oils

- **Lavender** calms your mind and body.
- **Ylang-ylang** encourages love and joy.
- **Sandalwood** grounds.
- **Jasmine** enhances intuition.
- **Frankincense** purifies and protects.
- **Myrrh** grounds and offers protection.
- **Rose** opens your heart to love.
- **Lemon balm** calms.
- **Clary sage** boots intuition.
- **Peppermint** refreshes.

In many traditions, the Moon symbolizes inner knowing, and mugwort and jasmine will further support this.

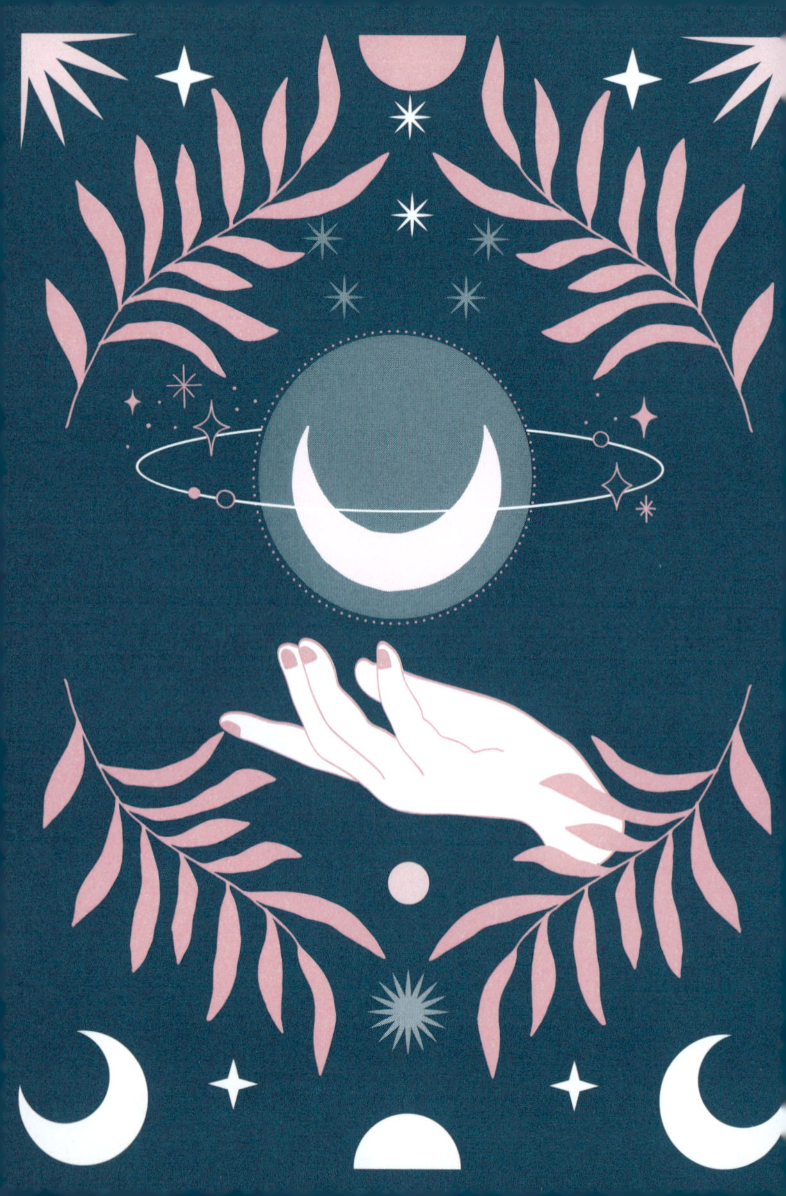

Chapter Three
MOON RITUALS

New Moon grounding ritual

This simple grounding ritual can be performed at any stage of the Moon cycle, but it is ideal for the New Moon as it helps you find balance before you work to manifest a new goal. If you simply want to connect with lunar energy to set a fresh intention, use a Moonstone crystal instead.

TOP TIP: Moon rituals can be practised throughout the lunar cycle or as stand-alone practices.

You'll need:

- White candle
- Matches
- Paper and pen
- Black Tourmaline crystal

MOON RITUALS

As the Moon goes through a monthly transformation, it is often used to symbolize change and renewal.

Ritual method

1. Settle down somewhere quiet or in front of your altar and carefully light your candle.

2. Set your intentions for this lunar cycle by reflecting on your goals. Write your intention on a piece of paper.

3. Sit quietly for a few minutes, holding the Black Tourmaline crystal in your lap. Focus on your breathing and imagine your body absorbing its grounding energy.

4. After a few minutes, or whenever you are ready, thank the crystal for its energy and carefully put out the candle.

5. Place the piece of paper with your intention on your altar or somewhere you can easily see it, as a reminder. If it is on a flat surface, place the crystal on top of your paper for the rest of this lunar cycle.

MOON RITUALS

To close each ritual (and spell) always thank the Moon for its guidance and support.

A planting ritual to grow your intention

The Waxing Crescent Moon is associated with growth and taking action, so it is the perfect phase to plant literal or metaphorical seeds!

This planting ritual is symbolic of nurturing your intention and your desire to see it through to fruition.

You'll need:

- Small pot
- Soil or compost
- Rosemary or lavender seeds
- Water

In many cultures, the Moon is associated with femininity and nurturing. In Mayan mythology, the Moon goddess Ixchel governs fertility, pregnancy and childbirth.

Ritual method

1. Find a calm, peaceful place to perform this ritual. You can do it indoors or better yet, outside under moonlight.

2. Fill two-thirds of your plant pot with soil or compost.

3. Hold your seed in your hand and recall your New Moon intention. If you didn't set one, focus on whatever it is in your life that you want to take root.

4. Carefully place the seed in the soil and imagine it growing to full size. Now speak your intention out loud and imagine your goal manifesting.

5. Fill the rest of the pot with the soil and lightly water the seed.

6. Position the plant pot on your altar or somewhere it will get enough sunlight. Place your written intention underneath the pot.

7. Care for your seed throughout the rest of the lunar cycle and enjoy watching the seedling grow!

A candle ritual for emotional balance

This candle ritual will help you balance your emotions – focusing on the flame can help you centre yourself.

It is ideal for the First Quarter Moon (which is about overcoming obstacles) but can be done at any phase of the lunar cycle.

You'll need:

- ✷ Blue candle
- ✷ Jasmine essential oil
- ✷ Matches
- ✷ Journal and pen

In astrology, a person's moon sign, which is determined by the Moon's position at the time of their birth, is believed to represent their true inner self.

Ritual method

1. Find a quiet area, such as in front of your altar, where you can sit quietly for at least ten minutes.

2. Anoint your candle with a few drops of jasmine oil.

3. Light the candle and rest your gaze softly on the flame – watch how it flickers as the wick burns and wax starts to melt.

4. Silently set your intention for the flame to help you find emotional balance.

MOON RITUALS

5. Relax here for up to ten minutes, breathing deeply while watching the flame.

6. If any thoughts come up that take away from your inner peace, visualize the flame absorbing and transforming them into calming energy.

7. When you are ready, extinguish the candle and take a moment to reflect or journal on any thoughts or feelings that came up during this ritual.

MOON MAGIC

A charm bag ritual for fertility

In this ritual, you fill a charm bag with special items to invite fertility of any kind into your life. It can be performed at any time, but it is especially potent during the Waxing Gibbous Moon.

You can adapt this ritual for an intention of abundance by changing the items you include.

You'll need:

- Green candle
- Jasmine incense
- Matches
- Small cloth bag, ideally green or pink
- Dried mugwort, nettle or red clover (or all!)
- Dried rose petals
- Small piece of Moonstone or Rose Quartz
- An item that represents fertility to you
- Your intention written on a piece of paper

The Moon sometimes represents dreams, because it is associated with the subconscious mind – making it a symbol of the mysterious world we enter while we sleep.

Ritual method

1. Sit quietly at your altar and light the green candle and jasmine incense. Let the scent of the incense fill your space and connect you with the nurturing, feminine energy of the Moon.

2. Take some calming deep breaths. Imagine drawing in the Moon's growing energy.

3. Mindfully place the items one by one into the charm bag. As you do so, focus deeply on your intention for fertility.

MOON RITUALS

4. Tie the charm bag tightly to secure everything inside.

5. Extinguish your candle and incense before you leave your sacred space.

6. Place the charm bag under your pillow. Sleep with it there for the rest of this lunar cycle and each night, touch the bag and reaffirm your intention for fertility.

Simple ritual for safe travel

Carry out this ritual at the Waxing Gibbous Moon or in the days before an upcoming journey. When you travel, take the crystal with you.

This ritual can be adapted to any situation that brings up nerves.

You'll need:

- ✳ A white candle
- ✳ Matches
- ✳ A journal and pen
- ✳ A Labradorite or Moonstone crystal

MOON RITUALS

> **"The Moon is faithful to its nature, and its power is never diminished."**
>
> Deng Ming-Dao,
> *Everyday Tao* (1996)

Ritual method

1. Sit comfortably by your altar or somewhere else peaceful. Light your candle and take a few deep breaths to centre yourself. Close your eyes and imagine an image of the Waxing Gibbous Moon.

2. Write your intention for safe travel on a blank page in your journal and set it out in front of you.

3. Lightly hold your crystal and visualize yourself surrounded by a bright white, protective light.

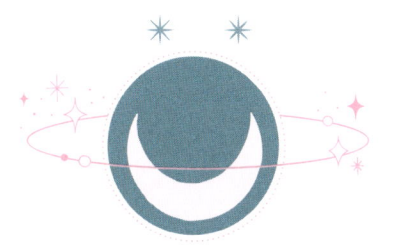

4. Imagine each stage of your journey, from packing and getting ready to when you safely arrive at your destination. Visualize everything working out perfectly. If you find it difficult to imagine things running smoothly, visualize kind people coming to help you at every stage.

5. Once you have finished, take some time to journal on anything that came up for you.

6. Keep the crystal with you throughout your journey, either in your pocket or bag, so it can represent the Moon's protective energy.

MOON MAGIC

Full Moon ritual for releasing heartbreak

The heightened energy of the Full Moon is an ideal moment to let go of lingering emotions from heartbreak.

If you can, charge the water you use as part of this ritual under the Moon for a few hours.

You'll need:

* A comforting item (optional)
* Pen and paper
* A small bowl of water (ideally charged under moonlight)
* Chamomile tea

Hecate, the Greek goddess of the Moon and magic, is often honoured during the Dark Moon, the period right before a New Moon, when her power to guide us through transitions is at its peak.

Ritual method

1. In a quiet, comfortable place, take some deep, calming breaths. If you feel apprehensive, hold an item – perhaps a crystal or a photo of a loved one – that brings you comfort.

2. Ground yourself by imagining roots growing from your feet deep into the Earth. Ask for support and imagine the tension leaving your body and travelling into the ground. With each breath, imagine pain or sadness (or whatever you feel) leaving your body.

3. Write a letter to the person who has hurt you, and don't hold back. Read it out loud to yourself as an act of acknowledgement that your feelings matter.

MOON RITUALS

4. Imagine moonlight pouring from the sky, gently soothing all the parts of you that hurt, then say out loud: "I release this heartbreak with love and compassion. I am open to healing."

5. Hold the bowl of water in your hands and imagine all the heartbreak being absorbed into the water. Visualize the water turning muddy with the energy that you are releasing. If you can, take the water outside and pour it onto the Earth.

6. Have a cup of soothing chamomile tea after this ritual and be gentle with yourself – this is deep, brave work.

Herbal tea ritual for emotional balance

This quiet, consciously meditative ritual invites you to slow down and connect with your internal world in a mindful way.

One evening during the Waning Gibbous Moon, step outside (or look out of the window) to gaze at the Moon, then find a quiet space where you can sit and connect with the introspective energy of this phase.

You'll need:

- Amethyst or Quartz crystals
- A handful of dried lemon balm leaves or shop-bought lemon balm tea bags
- Honey or lemon
- A teapot and hot water
- Your favourite mug
- A journal and pen (optional)

Ritual method

1. Choose a quiet place where you can sit and enjoy your tea. Wear comfy pyjamas, gather blankets, the crystals or any other items that soothe you. Set your intention to restore emotional balance by releasing whatever is disrupting your inner harmony.

2. As you prepare your tea, imagine that each step – pouring the water, steeping the leaves and stirring – helps you release negative energy. Move as slowly and as mindfully as you can.

MOON RITUALS

3. Let the tea brew for about five minutes then pour a cup.

4. When it is cool enough, focus on your breath and reflect on what you are releasing from your life with each sip. Take your time and write in your journal if you feel called to do so.

5. Once you have finished your drink, thank the leaves for supporting your wellbeing and get a good night's sleep.

Journaling ritual for self-reflection

During this ritual – ideally carried out at night during the Last Quarter Moon – reflect on the past lunar cycle, acknowledge what has and hasn't worked for you, and prepare for the following cycle.

You'll need:

- A white or silver candle
- Frankincense, myrrh or sandalwood incense
- Matches
- A journal and pen

Use this journaling ritual each month to face any ways you may have not acted in alignment with your intention, and with compassion, commit to moving forward with greater clarity.

Ritual method

1. In a quiet spot near a window, safely light the candle and incense of your choice. Let its scent fill your space and open the window to invite in fresh air and release the smoke.

2. Silently set your intention to reflect honestly on the past lunar cycle and welcome change.

3. Watch the incense burning – see how the smoke rises in twists and twirls. Imagine it carrying away anything you need to release up and out of the window.

MOON RITUALS

4. Open your journal and answer these prompts:

    * What lessons have I learned during this lunar cycle?
    * What challenges did I face?
    * How did I respond?
    * What do I need to release to move forward?
    * What are the next steps I can take toward personal growth?

5. As the incense burns out, write down anything else on your mind and close the ritual by extinguishing the candle.

Self-care foot massage ritual

The Waning Crescent Moon is a perfect opportunity to focus on self-care. It is a chance to release any lingering stress and honour your need for renewal before the next cycle.

You'll need:

- Sandalwood or other incense
- Matches
- Lavender or chamomile essential oil
- A carrier oil such as coconut oil or sweet almond oil
- A journal and pen

MOON RITUALS

The Waning Crescent lunar phase is a time for deep rest.

Ritual method

1. In a quiet space where you can relax, safely light your chosen incense.

2. Choose your oil and dilute a few drops in a carrier oil.

3. Take the time to massage your feet slowly and gently, focusing on your intention of self-care.

4. Use the time to reflect on these journal prompts:

    * What lingering emotions am I still holding on to?
    * How can I release these so that I can relax and prepare for the next lunar cycle?

5. Wash your hands, and then write down your answers in your journal.

Finish this ritual by writing:

I release all that weighs me down and holds me back. I honour my need for rest. I always do my best and I am enough.

And so it is, and so it was, and so it shall be.

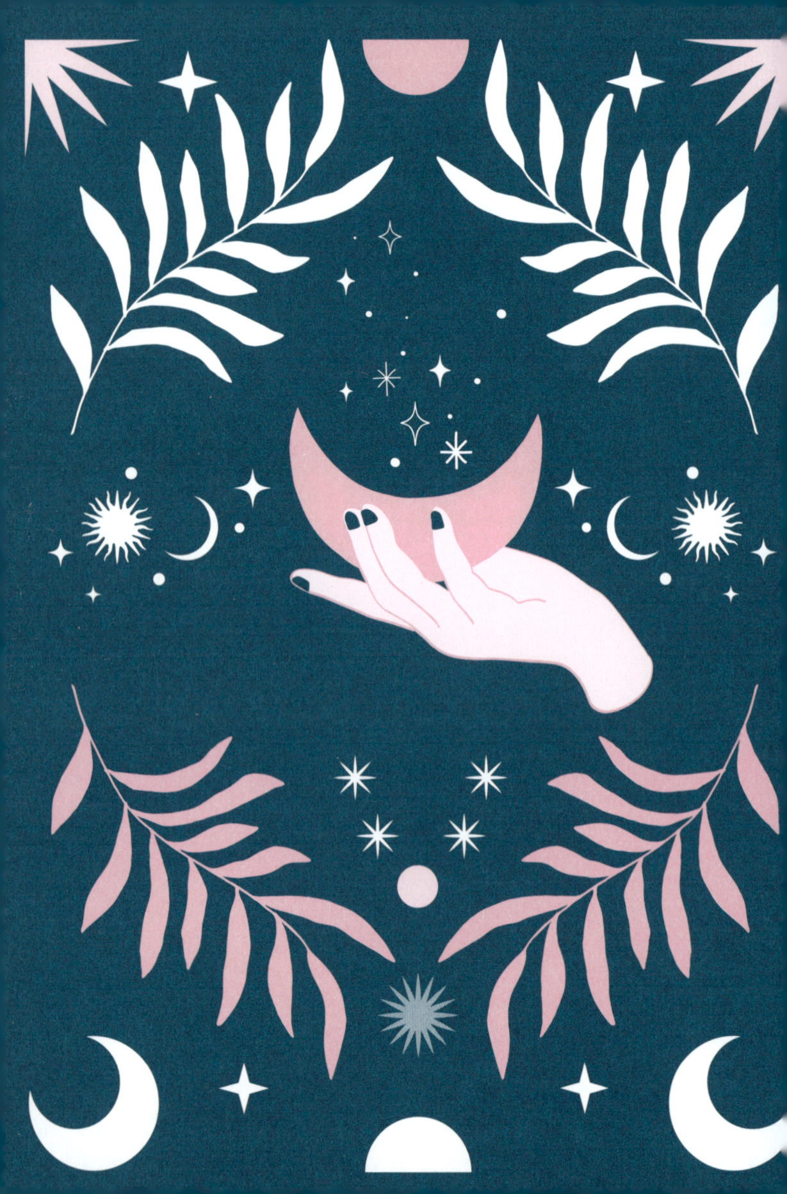

Chapter Four

LUNAR SPELLS

A spell is a statement spoken with energy, intention, focus and belief – a clear request to the Universe.

LUNAR SPELLS

New Moon spell for love

During the New Moon, the dark sky represents a fresh start – the perfect time to attract a new love!

You'll need:

- ✳ Piece of paper and pen
- ✳ A pink candle
- ✳ Rose essential oil
- ✳ Matches

TOP TIP: By aligning your spell work with the Moon's cycles, you can amplify your intentions.

Spell method

1. Write down on paper the qualities you desire in a partner. Be as detailed as you can.

2. Hold the paper in your hands, close your eyes and imagine what it would feel like to experience a person like this in your life. Let yourself feel the excitement and love as you do so.

3. Anoint the pink candle with rose oil, light it, and as the flame burns, imagine yourself with a partner who embodies your desires.

LUNAR SPELLS

Now, speak these spell words out loud:

"By the power of this New Moon's growing light,
I summon new love so pure, so bright.
I call forth one who mirrors my heart's desire,
Whose soul ignites my inner fire.
May I embody all the traits I seek,
In myself, may love grow strong, not weak.
Let this union, pure and free,
Arrive by will, as meant to be.
With open heart, I welcome thee,
So it is, and so shall it be."

MOON MAGIC

Vision board spell for abundance

The Waxing Crescent Moon is the perfect time for attracting abundance in all its forms.

This spell invites you to create a vision board that works as a magical tool to manifest prosperity.

LUNAR SPELLS

You'll need:

- A green candle
- Matches
- Citrine or Pyrite crystals
- Large piece of card
- Magazines, photos, newspapers or printed images representing abundance
- Scissors
- Glue

Spell method

1. In a quiet space, safely light your green candle and place your crystals nearby.

2. Close your eyes, take some deep breaths and focus on the abundance you wish to add to your life. Perhaps you desire increased finances or rich life experiences.

3. Speak out loud:

    "As the Moon grows, so too will my abundance. I open myself to receive [whatever it is you wish to manifest] or something that is even more nourishing. I am open to receiving all forms of abundance."

4. Create your vision board by cutting, arranging and sticking words and images on the board. As you place each item, visualize whatever it represents already being present in your life. Let yourself feel the joy of abundance.

5. When your board is complete, hold your hands over it, close your eyes and visualize a soft green light charging it. Say out loud:

   "I charge this board with power and might, to bring my desires into the light."

6. Place your board somewhere you will see it throughout the coming month and each time you look at it, acknowledge it with a nod and consciously feel abundance moving toward you.

7. Soon after you create your board, you may notice subconscious resistance arising. Release this by saying:

   "I see you, I honour you and now I release you. I am worthy of abundance."

A First Quarter Moon spell for healing

In this spell, the moonlight-charged water is a symbolic vehicle for healing energy.

You'll need:

- A light blue candle
- Matches
- A piece of paper and pen
- Rose Quartz
- A sprig of lavender
- Lavender essential oil
- A small bowl of water charged by moonlight

In Hinduism, Chandra, the god of the Moon is also known as Soma. He governs the night and plants.

Spell method

1. Sitting at your altar, take a few moments to think about the area of your life or your body that needs healing.

2. Close your eyes and imagine yourself surrounded by a pale blue light. Place your candle at the centre of your altar and light it safely.

3. Now write your intention on a piece of paper: "I am healing. Peace and love surround me."

4. Place your intention, the Rose Quartz crystal and lavender sprig on your altar. Use your intuition to decide where to place them.

5. Add a few drops of essential oil to the water and then place the bowl on top of your intention.

LUNAR SPELLS

6. Say out loud:

   "With this water, I heal, cleanse and restore. And so it is, and so it was, and so it shall be."

7. Sit for a few moments, still imagining the blue light around you. Visualize it growing in strength and expanding outward.

8. When you feel ready, put out the candle and imagine your intention being sent out into the Universe. Repeat this spell throughout the lunar cycle if you wish.

Just like crystals and water, you can charge bay leaves under moonlight.

LUNAR SPELLS

Candle spell for career success

Here's a simple spell for boosting your career during the Waxing Gibbous Moon, aligning with the energy of building momentum and success.

You'll need:

- Citrine and Clear Quartz crystals
- A piece of paper and pen
- Cinnamon or basil essential oil
- A gold candle
- Matches
- Fireproof dish
- Dried bay leaves

Spell method

1. Find a quiet place, such as in front of your altar, to perform your spell.

2. Take a few deep breaths and focus on your career goals as you hold the crystals. Write your intention on a piece of paper.

3. Rub a few drops of the essential oil onto your candle from the base to the wick. Imagine the candle being infused with your career desires, and then light it.

4. Carefully light your written intention with the candle flame and let it burn in the fireproof dish to release its energy into the Universe.

5. Write words associated with your desires, such as "success" or "recognition" on the bay leaves and carefully burn them, too. Bay leaves have long been associated with protection and manifestation.

6. Put out the candle and bury the ash in the dish outdoors to complete your spell.

7. For added power, keep the crystals at your workspace for the rest of the lunar cycle.

Full Moon spell for cutting cords

The Full Moon is a potent time for cutting cords with unhealthy attachments connected to emotions, relationships or situations that no longer serve you.

You'll need:

- Your favourite dried herbs or incense for cleansing
- A Clear Quartz crystal
- A white candle
- A black candle
- Matches
- Some string
- Scissors
- A bowl of water

A simple banishing ritual involves placing two rocks far apart to represent distance between two things that you wish to disconnect.

Spell method

1. Cleanse yourself and your space using dried herbs or incense before starting this spell (*see page 43*).

2. Sit comfortably holding your crystal and imagine yourself connected to whatever or whoever you wish to cut cords.

3. Light both candles, then take the string in your hand, while continuing to imagine the energetic cord in your mind.

4. Now, speak out loud:

   "Under this Full Moon, I cut the cords that bind me. I now reclaim my energy. I am free."

5. Imagine the cord being cut in your mind, then physically cut the string with scissors, as a symbolic act of release. Some people may physically feel where the cord was attached to their body. If you experience this, gently "pull" out the cords using your hands until you sense a release. Afterwards, rub the area gently to soothe, and close the space where the attachment once was.

6. To finish, wash your hands lightly in the bowl of water, put out the candles and bury the pieces of string outdoors.

As it waxes and wanes, the Moon is sometimes associated with illusion as it shows how things may change or be perceived differently.

LUNAR SPELLS

Candle spell to amplify gratitude

This simple candle spell uses the energy of the Waning Gibbous Moon to amplify your gratitude, sending it into the Universe to attract even more blessings.

You'll need:

- ✳ Yellow candle
- ✳ Matches
- ✳ Piece of paper
- ✳ Purple pen or pencil
- ✳ Fireproof dish

Spell method

1. In a quiet space, light your candle and say out loud:

   "With this flame, I honour the blessings that I have received. I give thanks as the lunar cycle ends."

2. On the paper, write down three things that you are grateful for from the last month. Allow the lovely feeling of deep appreciation to flow through you. After each point, write:

   "I give thanks for this blessing, may it take root and grow."

3. Hold the paper and visualize a bright golden light surrounding your words – imagine this energy of gratitude expanding outwards into the Universe.

4. Carefully light the paper in the candle flame, allowing it to burn completely in the fireproof dish. Once it has turned to ash, say:

   "As I give thanks, I make space for even more to grow."

Burning spell for letting go

Here's a simple and powerful Last Quarter Moon spell using bay leaves to help you let go of negativity. Ideally, perform this spell outside under moonlight.

You'll need:

- Smoky Quartz
- Dried bay leaves
- Pen
- Fireproof dish
- Matches

LUNAR SPELLS

The Moon rules the zodiac sign of Cancer because both symbolize emotional depth, intuition and nurturing energy.

Spell method

1. Somewhere quiet – ideally outdoors under moonlight – hold your crystal and focus on the energy of the Last Quarter Moon.

2. Write on the bay leaves the things you want to release.

3. Hold each leaf over your fireproof dish and carefully light it.

4. As each one burns, imagine the thing you're releasing dissolving with the smoke.

5. Say out loud:

   "I release this [emotion, situation or person] from my life. I am open to new beginnings."

6. Once all the leaves have turned to ash, you can either bury the ash or dispose of it in a river or stream.

7. Finish off by doing some barefoot grounding (*see page 47*).

According to some Indigenous Australian traditions, the Moon is said to have once been a thin man who gradually becomes full as the Moon reaches its peak.

LUNAR SPELLS

Jar spell for releasing

The Waning Crescent Moon is the perfect time for a releasing spell, allowing you to let go of anything that no longer serves you as the Moon prepares for a new cycle.

You'll need:
- A few dried bay leaves
- A small handful of sea salt
- A Black Obsidian crystal
- Paper and pen
- A clean, empty jam jar
- Black thread
- Frankincense essential oil
- A tealight candle
- Matches

Spell method

1. Somewhere quiet, take a few deep breaths and focus on what you want to release at this final Moon phase. Write your intention on the piece of paper.

2. Place the bay leaves, salt, crystal and paper into the jar. Put the lid on the jar and then wrap the thread around it several times.

3. Say out loud:

   "With this thread, I bind my intention. I deeply and completely release my fear of failure. And so it is, and so it was, and so it shall be."

LUNAR SPELLS

4. Add a few drops of the essential oil to the candle, then light it and place it safely on top of the jar. As it burns, imagine the flame burning away whatever you are releasing.

5. Bury the jar outdoors to symbolize permanent release.

6. To add strength to this ritual, let the candle burn until it goes out on its own.

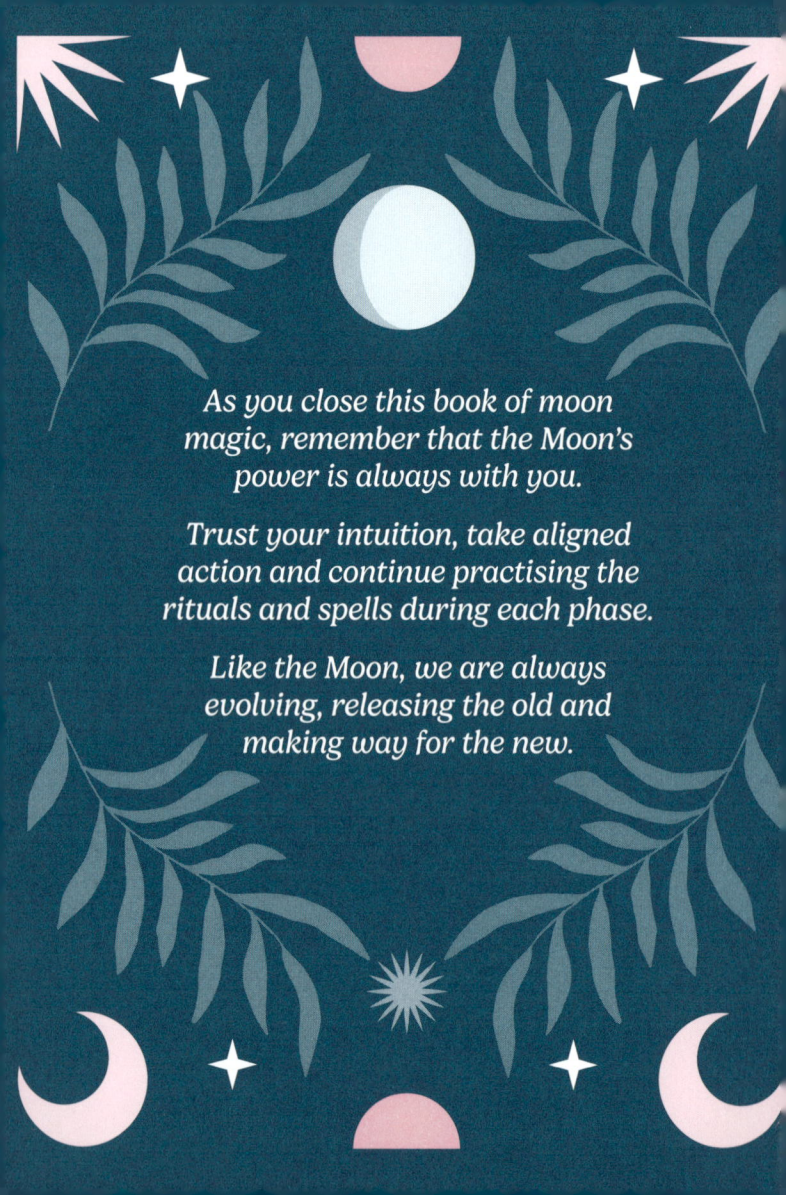

As you close this book of moon magic, remember that the Moon's power is always with you.

Trust your intuition, take aligned action and continue practising the rituals and spells during each phase.

Like the Moon, we are always evolving, releasing the old and making way for the new.